Text

What is Literary Non-fiction?

Charlotte Guillain

Raintree is an imprint of Capstone Global Library Limited, a company incorporated in England and Wales having its registered office at 7 Pilgrim Street, London, EC4V 6LB – Registered company number: 6695582

www.raintree.co.uk
myorders@raintree.co.uk

Text © Capstone Global Library Limited 2016
The moral rights of the proprietor have been asserted.

Edited by Clare Lewis and Penny West
Designed by Philippa Jenkins and Tim Bond
Picture research by Gina Kammer
Originated by Capstone Global Library Ltd
Produced by Helen McCreath
Printed and bound by CTPS

ISBN 978 1 406 29683 9
19 18 17 16 15
10 9 8 7 6 5 4 3 2 1

British Library Cataloguing in Publication Data
A full catalogue record for this book is available from the British Library.

Acknowledgements
We would like to thank the following for permission to reproduce photographs:
Alamy: © razorpix, 19; Capstone Studio: Karon Dubke, 7, 8, 16, 17, 20, 21, 22; Corbis: © Bettmann, 26; Getty Images: Agence France Presse, 6, Print Collector, 9; Landov: dpa/KATJA LENZ, 12; Library of Congress, 27; Newscom: EPA/JON HRUSA, 19, Jamie Grill Blend Images/JGI, 29, Photoshot/Starstock/Jonathon Short, 10, ZUMAPRESS/Henglein And Steets, 4; Shutterstock: Andresr, 15, Anneka, 5, ikeriderlondon, 28, Blend Images, 24, Catalin Petolea, 25, Robnroll, 13, Ryan Rodrick Beiler, 11

Contents

A world of non-fiction... 4

What is literary non-fiction? 6

What types of literary non-fiction are there? 8

Who writes literary non-fiction? 10

Why do people read literary non-fiction? 12

What are the features of literary non-fiction? ... 14

Pictures in literary non-fiction 16

Autobiography 18

How to write literary non-fiction:
Starting an autobiography 20

Biography and historical writing................. 22

How to write literary non-fiction:
Retelling an event in history 24

Speeches 26

How to write literary non-fiction:
Writing a speech 28

Glossary... 30

Find out more 31

Index 32

Some words are shown in bold, **like this**. You can find out what they mean by looking in the glossary.

A world of non-fiction

We read for many different reasons. We read websites and newspapers to find out what is going on in the world. We read stories, poems and comics to discover new worlds and imaginary characters who can show us all kinds of adventures. There are two main types of text that we read: **fiction** and **non-fiction**.

We read non-fiction on posters and signs to help us find our way around.

Ask your friends to recommend something you wouldn't normally read and see if you like it.

Fiction is writing that has been completely made up by the writer. It has characters and a story from the writer's imagination. Non-fiction is not made up. It is about facts – real things that have happened. Non-fiction gives us the information we need as we go through our lives. Non-fiction can be articles in magazines or the instructions for a new computer game. The information books you find in your school library are non-fiction. This book is about **literary non-fiction**.

Text around you

Do you prefer reading fiction or non-fiction? Try reading a type of text that you would never normally pick up. You might be surprised how much you enjoy it!

What is literary non-fiction?

Literary non-fiction is sometimes called creative non-fiction. It is the closest type of **non-fiction** to **fiction** because of the language and style of the writing. Unlike other types of non-fiction, literary non-fiction tries to affect the reader's senses and emotions. This means the writer might create a lot of descriptive text that uses **adjectives** and **adverbs**. He or she could also use language with features such as **similes**, **metaphors** and **alliteration**. All of these make writing more colourful and appealing.

Martin Luther King made a famous speech in 1963 calling for peace and equality for all Americans. In his speech he used many metaphors, such as "the solid rock of brotherhood" and "the valley of despair".

Literary non-fiction is usually written in the **past tense** and the **third person**. **Autobiographies** and personal accounts are written in the **first person** as the writer is describing his or her own life.

Text tips!

If you're writing a piece of literary non-fiction text, think about how you can make your writing more colourful. You don't just want to write the bare facts. Instead, you should appeal to your reader's senses and include some exciting description.

What types of literary non-fiction are there?

Examples of **literary non-fiction** include:

- Speeches
- **Biographies** about famous people's lives
- **Autobiographies** about the author's own life
- Travel writing about the author's experiences in different parts of the world
- Essays on a range of subjects
- **Eyewitness accounts** of important events
- Articles in magazines and newspapers.

A biography is a piece of writing about a person's life and work.

These types of text are found in printed books and in digital formats. People usually read literary non-fiction **chronologically**. This means that they start reading at the beginning and work through the book to the end. It wouldn't normally make sense to dip straight into the middle of the book and start reading.

Literary non-fiction contains accurate information and lots of details about the people, place and time being described. The writer writes in a way that will hook the reader in so they want to keep reading to the end.

Text in history

Some of the most famous books ever written are literary non-fiction. Charles Darwin's book about the natural world, *On the Origin of Species*, was published in 1859. Many scientists have presented new ideas in works of literary non-fiction throughout history.

Who writes literary non-fiction?

People who write **literary non-fiction** know a lot about their subject. Often they are writing about personal experiences, for example their life and work, in an **autobiography**. They may write about a journey they took in a piece of travel writing. Other writers of literary non-fiction are specialists in a subject they've studied. They might be scientists or other experts. They have done a lot of research and want to share what they've learned with a wider audience.

Lots of people enjoy reading travel writing because they can learn about different parts of the world without travelling anywhere!

Important speeches are carefully written by experts.

Other literary non-fiction is written by journalists. They write articles and essays about important events or people. Some people write literary non-fiction online, on blogs or websites. Speeches are written for important people to give at special events. The best speeches are often written down for people to read afterwards and this is another type of literary non-fiction.

Text tips!

If you're going to write a piece of literary non-fiction, choose your subject carefully. It needs to be something you know a lot about, unless you have lots of time to research something new!

Why do people read literary non-fiction?

Many people enjoy reading **literary non-fiction**. If you're interested in a particular subject, it can be fascinating to read what an expert has written about it. Lots of readers like to read **biographies** of famous people to learn more about their lives. Some people like to read travel writing before they visit a new place. This helps them to learn more about the history of the country and the people who live there.

People like reading literary non-fiction because they enjoy the style and language that the writer uses. Many readers like the way literary non-fiction gives them information but is written in a way that is similar to **fiction**. Today many people get a lot of information from the internet. They like to read literary non-fiction, such as articles and **eyewitness accounts**, online.

Text in history

If you're interested in history, you might enjoy *A Little History of the World* by Ernst Gombrich. He wrote this book in 1935, taking the reader through human history from the Stone Age onwards.

Lots of literary
non-fiction is
available on
the internet.

What are the features of literary non-fiction?

Literary non-fiction can include the following features:

- This type of **non-fiction** often looks very similar to **fiction**. Literary non-fiction can be divided up into chapters and the writer will often use similar language to fiction.

- The reader is usually supposed to read a piece of literary non-fiction from start to finish. Reading literary non-fiction is like reading a story. It has a clear beginning and end, and there are exciting and dramatic moments.

- The writing in a piece of literary non-fiction will move towards a clear ending.

- This sort of non-fiction text might have **appendices** that give extra information at the back of the book. There might be an **index**, too.

- Like many other types of non-fiction, literary non-fiction tends to use a lot of time connectives, such as "first", "next", "meanwhile" and "afterwards".

Text around you

Look in your school or local library for a **biography** of a person who interests you. Can you spot any typical features of literary non-fiction? Is the book divided into chapters like a **novel**?

Reading about a famous person's life can be fascinating.

Pictures in literary non-fiction

Writers often add images to **non-fiction** text. These add interest and give more information. Some **literary non-fiction** is illustrated and can look a lot like **fiction**.

A lot of literary non-fiction includes photographs that show the people, things and places described in the text. In **biographies** and **autobiographies** it is interesting for the reader to see pictures of the person the book is about at different stages of their life.

Text around you

Find some examples of literary non-fiction in your library. Flick through the books and see what sort of pictures and graphics are included. What do you think they add to the book?

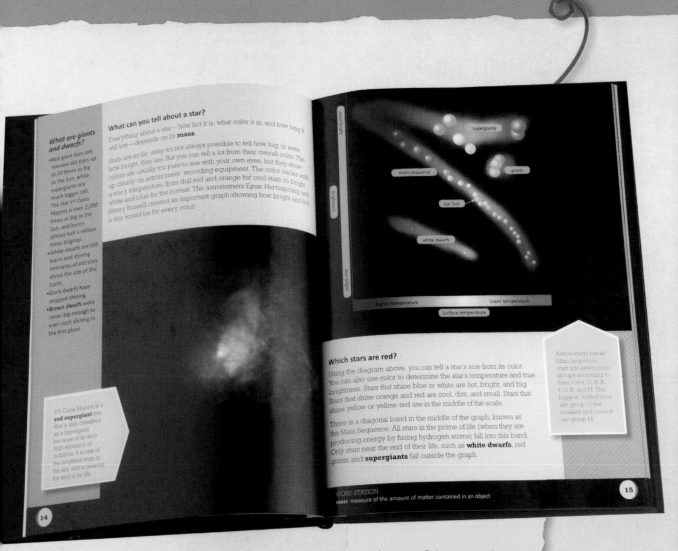

It's useful to see this
information about
the colour of stars, as
well as read about it.

Travel writers often include photographs of places
they have visited. Their writing usually includes
maps showing routes taken by the writer and
important locations. Scientific writing and other
academic literary non-fiction can be full of graphs
and charts. These show the results of research in a
quick and clear way.

Autobiography

An **autobiography** is a piece of **literary non-fiction** that the author writes about his or her own life and achievements. Famous people often write autobiographies because many people are interested in their lives and how they became well known.

The South African leader Nelson Mandela wrote about his life in his autobiography *Conversations with Myself.*

Autobiographies can have the following features:

- The text is broken up into sections or chapters.
- The writer takes the reader through the stages of their life, usually in **chronological** order.
- They often include personal details and memories.
- They might include photos of different parts of the writer's life.
- Autobiographies are likely to focus on the part of his or her life that the writer is best known for.

Text in history

Roald Dahl (1916–1990) wrote two autobiographies. The first, *Boy: Tales of Childhood*, is about his early life and time at school. *Going Solo* is about his life as a grown-up before he became a writer, including his experiences as a pilot in World War II (1939–1945).

How to write literary non-fiction: Starting an autobiography

Many **autobiographies** start with the writer's first memory. Why not write about your earliest memory to share with your friends and family?

1. Think about your childhood and look at photos of when you were little. What early memories can you remember?

2. Choose one memory and make notes about it. Have you got all the information about the event, such as the date, the place and your age at the time?

3. Start to write your memory in a first **draft**. Write in the **first person** and **past tense**. Try to describe the events in the order that they happened.

4. Go through your first draft. Make your writing more interesting with **adjectives** or **adverbs**. Use **similes** or **metaphors** to help the reader to picture what you are describing. Tell the reader how you were feeling at the time.

5. Can you add any useful time connectives, such as "next", "afterwards" or "meanwhile"? This helps to make the sequence of events clearer.

6. Check your spelling and grammar!

7. Write or type up a final version of your memory and share it with a friend or family member. Add photos if you like.

Biography and historical writing

A **biography** is also about a person's life or part of his or her life. However, it is written by someone else – a biographer. The biographer has to research the person's life, either by interviewing the person themselves or people who knew them. The biographer also studies letters, diaries and other information.

People who write about historical events have to do similar research to biographers. They spend a lot of time finding out accurate information. They try not to be influenced by other writers' opinions about events.

How many biographies have you read?

Text around you

Ask your librarian if he or she can recommend any biographies about someone you're interested in. Or you could look for biographies of people involved in something that interests you, such as sport or science. Does reading about the person help you to understand their achievements?

Biographies and historical writing often have the following features:

- Presentation of the events in **chronological** order, as they happened.
- Quotations from letters, diaries and other written sources.
- The writer's own opinions or judgements about the subject and why things happened the way they did.
- Photos, maps and other illustrations.

How to write literary non-fiction:
Retelling an event in history

Write about an historical event that happened in your local area.

1. Talk to a relative or a teacher to help you choose an event. Think of some questions about what happened. Write the questions down and leave space for the answers.

2. It's time to research the answers! Check library books and the internet. Only visit websites that provide information you can trust, such as those of museums and important organizations. You could also visit a museum or other historical site.

3. Note down your findings in the space beneath each question.

4. Now plan how you are going to structure your writing. You'll need an **introduction** and a **conclusion**. Make sure you include details about dates, places and people.

5. Use your notes to write up your text in your own words. Make sure the facts you found in different places match up – otherwise you'll need to do more research to get the right answers!

6. Check your spelling and grammar and make sure that you've written the text in the correct order.

7. Add photos or maps to make the text even more interesting.

8. Share your writing with your family, friends or teacher.

Speeches

People write speeches for other people to hear. Many important speeches are written down for people to read afterwards, too. Some speeches, such as Martin Luther King's "I Have a Dream" speech, have become very famous.

In the United States, Susan B. Anthony (1820–1906) used memorable speeches to help win the right to vote for women.

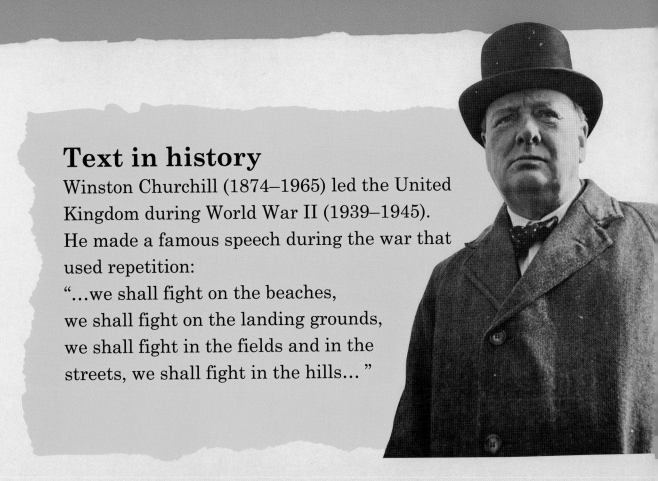

Text in history

Winston Churchill (1874–1965) led the United Kingdom during World War II (1939–1945). He made a famous speech during the war that used repetition:

"...we shall fight on the beaches, we shall fight on the landing grounds, we shall fight in the fields and in the streets, we shall fight in the hills... "

Many good speeches have some of the following features:

- Words or phrases are repeated so they stick in the listener or reader's mind. Martin Luther King repeated "Let freedom ring..." in his speech.
- They sometimes include **rhetorical questions**. These questions don't expect an answer but they make the listener think about what the speaker is saying.
- A speech often talks to the listener or reader directly. It tries to persuade them to a certain point of view or appeal to their feelings.
- Speeches may include **anecdotes**.
- There are often longer sentences followed by shorter sentences, which stand out.

How to write literary non-fiction: Writing a speech

Write a speech about something you really care about.

1. Pick a subject that really matters to you for your speech. For example, you could talk about why it is so important to look after pets properly.

2. Start by introducing yourself and your subject. Explain why this subject matters to you.

3. Break your speech up into different points. When you have written about each point, give examples to show why it matters. You could include personal stories about your own experience.

4. Can you repeat some words or phrases to get your listener's attention?

5. Include some **rhetorical questions** – these are questions you ask when you don't really expect an answer. They just make the listener think.

6. Include some short, snappy sentences after a few long ones. These add variety and make the speech sound more interesting.

7. Write a good **conclusion** to your speech. It should stick in the reader's mind and persuade them that your ideas are right!

8. When you've finished writing your speech, practise reading it. When you are ready, read it out loud to your family and friends!

Glossary

adjective word that describes a noun

adverb word that describes a verb

alliteration when words start with the same first letter

anecdote personal story

appendix (plural: appendices) extra information at the end of a book

autobiography story of the writer's life

biography story of someone else's life

chronological in the order that things happened

conclusion ending to a piece of writing

draft early attempt at a piece of writing

eyewitness account story of real events told by someone who was there

fiction story that's not true

first person when a writer uses "I" and "me"

index list of words in a book with page numbers where you will find that word

introduction beginning of a piece of writing that explains what the writing will be about

literary non-fiction writing that uses literary techniques usually used in fiction to report on real-life events

metaphor when something is described as being another thing

non-fiction writing about real-life facts

novel long story

past tense writing that describes events that have already happened

rhetorical question question asked to have an impact on the reader or listener; it doesn't normally expect an answer

simile when one thing is compared to another

third person when a writer talks about "her", "him" or "they"

Find out more

To learn more about literary non-fiction in all its forms, take a look at the following books. These include examples of biography, autobiography and historical events. You could also use the websites listed below to research a subject that interests you. Use your findings and the "How to" topics in this book to test out your new literary non-fiction writing skills!

Books

A Little History of the World, Ernst Gombrich (Yale University Press, 2008)

Boy: Tales of Childhood, Roald Dahl (Puffin, 2013)

Charles Darwin (Science Biographies), Nick Hunter (Raintree, 2015)

Going Solo, Roald Dahl (Puffin, 2013)

Long Walk to Freedom, Nelson Mandela, abridged by Chris van Wyk (Macmillan Children's Books, 2010)

Martin Luther King (Inspirational Lives), Jen Green (Wayland, 2014)

Websites

www.bbc.co.uk/newsround/25262272
You can hear some of Nelson Mandela's most famous speeches on this BBC website.

www.theguardian.com/theguardian/series/greatspeeches
You can read and hear some more great speeches, including those made by Martin Luther King and Winston Churchill, on this website.

www.roalddahl.com
Find out more about Roald Dahl's life on this website about the writer and his books.

Index

adjectives 6, 21
adverbs 6, 21
alliteration 6
anecdotes 27
Anthony, Susan B. 26
appendices 14
autobiographies 7, 8, 10,
  16, 18–21

biographies 8, 12, 15, 16,
  22, 23

chapters 14, 15, 19
chronological order 9, 19,
  23
Churchill, Winston 27
conclusions 25, 29
connectives 14, 21
creative non-fiction 6

Dahl, Roald 19
Darwin, Charles 9
drafts 20, 21

essays 8, 11
eyewitness accounts 8, 12

features 14
fiction 4, 5, 6, 14, 16
first person 7, 20

game instructions 5
Gombrich, Ernst 12
graphs and charts 17

historical writing 12,
  22–23, 24–25

indexes 14
introductions 25, 28

journalists 11

King, Martin Luther 6, 26,
  27

language 6, 12, 14
libraries 5
literary non-fiction: what
  it is 6–7

magazine and newspaper
  articles 5, 8, 11
Mandela, Nelson 18
maps 23, 25
metaphors 6, 21

non-fiction 4, 5

online texts 11, 12, 13

past tense 7, 20
pictures 16–17, 19, 21, 23,
  25

quotations 23

repetition 27, 29
rhetorical questions 27, 29

senses and emotions 6, 7
similes 6, 21
specialist subjects 10, 11,
  12
speeches 6, 8, 11, 26–29
spelling and grammar 21,
  25

third person 7
travel writing 8, 10, 12, 17
types of literary non-fiction 8–9

websites 11, 24
writers 10–11